BEYOND CONSULTING

BEYOND CONSULTING

Empowering Your Practice

Unlock Your Potential with 5 Essential Strategies
to enhance OPD & Strengthen Patient Relationships

Kuljive Mahajan

Worldwide Published by
Pendown Press

PENDOWN PRESS LLP

An ISO 9001 & ISO 14001 Certified Co.,

Regd. Office: 3767A, Kanhaiya Nagar,

Tri Nagar, Delhi-110035

Ph.: 8130886000, 9650072927

E-mail: info@pendownpress.com

Branch Office: 1A/2A, 20, Hari Sadan, Ansari Road,

Daryaganj, New Delhi-110002

Ph.: 011-45794768

Website: PendownPress.com

Edition: 2024

Price: ₹ 297/-

ISBN: 978-93-6338-541-2

Layout and Cover Designed by Pendown Graphics Team
Printed and Bound in India by Thomson Press India Ltd.

Dedicated to my family and team.

Without their understanding, support and love, the completion of this book would not have been possible.

GRATITUDE

My sincere gratitude to all the Doctors for trusting
CONSERN with their unwavering support. Your
confidence in our mission and products fuels
our commitment to excellence and drives
our continuous effort to innovate and
serve the healthcare community better.

Contents

Preface

Healthcare is no longer just about healing; it's a complex business demanding strategic acumen. As the saying goes, "If you fail to plan, you plan to fail." Nowhere is this truer than in the realm of patient acquisition. In a world where change is the only constant, a proactive approach to expanding your patient base is not merely an option, but a necessity.

My journey through the pharmaceutical industry has opened my eyes to the transformative power of a well-executed patient acquisition strategy. It's about more than just numbers; it's about improving lives. It's about ensuring that the right care reaches the right people at the right time.

This book is your roadmap to unlocking that potential. It's a compilation of insights, strategies, and real-world examples designed to equip you with the tools to grow your practice or organization. Whether you're a seasoned healthcare professional or just starting out, you'll find valuable guidance within these pages.

Let's embark on this journey together. Let's redefine the landscape of healthcare, one patient at a time.

Remember, as the legendary business magnate, Henry Ford, once said,

> *"Coming together is a beginning. Keeping together is progress. Working together is success."*

Introduction

Did you know that healthcare practices with a strategic growth plan see a 20% increase in patient retention?

Yes, yes, you heard it right!

But the question arises: How can you achieve such impressive results?

In today's ever-evolving healthcare landscape, the value of a structured effort to expand your patient base cannot be underestimated. My experience in the pharma industry has given me new insights into the transformative power of these efforts to reshape the growth curve. This book is designed to help you unlock that potential and harness this power for your practice, ensuring sustainable growth and success.

We will learn more about it in the upcoming pages, but first...

I am Kuljive Mahajan, a first-generation entrepreneur with over 28 years of experience in the pharma industry. Starting from humble beginnings in a middle-class family, I learned early the values of hard work, integrity, and excellence. These values steered my entrepreneurial journey, leading to the establishment of *Consern Pharma Limited.* Today, Consern is a recognized name in the CNS segment, partnering with over 9,700 specialist doctors across India.

Consern Pharma Limited is not just another pharmaceutical company; it is certified by WHO-GMP and ZED Gold, and boasts its own in-house DSIR-certified R&D unit approved by the Government of India. Our journey from a modest start to filing over 110 patents is a testament to our commitment to innovation and excellence.

Purpose of This Book

The idea of writing this book was born from a desire to share the insights and strategies that have significantly contributed to our success. It is crafted for healthcare professionals looking to enhance their Outpatient Department (OPD) services, streamline operations, and foster deeper connections with their patients.

what you will get?

By the end of this book, you will be equipped with:

➢ **Proven strategies** to expand and optimize your OPD operations, making your practice more accessible and inviting.

➢ **Tools and insights** to build a stronger bond with your patients, thus increasing patient retention and satisfaction.

➢ **Actionable tips** on leveraging digital marketing to enhance your practice's visibility and attract new patients.

➢ **Strategies on personalized patient care** that will set you apart in a competitive healthcare landscape.

Welcome to a journey of growth, innovation, and success. Together, let's enhance healthcare delivery and make a lasting impact in the lives of those we serve.

Chapter - 1

Unlock the Power of Consultancy

In the early stages of medical practice, consultants often juggle multiple roles. Initially, the temptation is to wear multiple hats — from managing patient consultations to overseeing administrative tasks and ensuring compliance management. While such multitasking is a common start-up strategy, it can dilute the consultant's focus and compromise the quality of patient care.

The Crucial Role of Specialization

The value of specialization cannot be underestimated. According to research by the American Medical Association, physicians spend more time on administrative duties than they do with patients. This imbalance highlights the necessity for dedicated roles within your practice, such as:

➢ **Clinic Manager:** Tasked with daily operations, human resources, and compliance, this role is pivotal in unburdening the medical staff from non-clinical duties.

➢ **Medical Assistant:** Plays a supportive role in managing patient flow, checking vitals like monitoring BP, temperature, weight, etc., handling preliminary medical documentation, and following up on consultations.

Establishing these specialized roles allows medical professionals to dedicate their time and expertise where it matters most—direct patient care.

Leveraging Technology for Efficiency

Incorporating technology to automate routine tasks can significantly enhance operational efficiency. The following tools are highly recommended for medical practices:

➢ **Electronic Health Records (EHR):** Maintaining electronic health records of patients is invaluable for streamlining patient information management, reducing reliance on physical paperwork and improving the accessibility of medical records.

➢ **Appointment Scheduling Software:** Tools such as Calendly or Practo offer automation of appointment bookings, confirmations, and reminders, thus mitigating administrative overhead and reducing patient no-shows.

➢ **Task Management Systems:** Software or digital apps provide a structured way to manage operational tasks, keeping all team members aligned and accountable.

Establishing Effective Systems

Creating a systematic approach to practice management involves more than adopting new tools; it requires a cultural shift towards consistent and reliable workflows. Here are steps to achieve this:

1. **Develop Clear Protocols:** Documenting standard operating procedures (SOPs) is essential for ensuring that every aspect of your clinic operates consistently and efficiently.

2. **Create Training Resources:** Developing comprehensive training videos and manuals can facilitate efficient onboarding and continuous training of staff, minimizing the need for direct intervention from the medical professionals.

3. **Delegate Appropriately:** Begin by outsourcing non-critical tasks. As your practice grows and resources allow, transition these responsibilities in-house, assigning them to specialized personnel.

Empowering Your Practice
Through Delegation

The transition from a do-it-all approach to a delegation model is pivotal. This not only enhances operational efficiency but profoundly improves the quality of patient care. By delegating non-medical tasks to capable hands, you'll find more time to focus on what you trained for i.e. caring for your patients.

The more streamlined your processes, the more your practice can handle, allowing for growth without sacrificing the quality of care. This setup not only supports the current state of your practice but also lays a robust foundation for future expansion.

Conclusion

Adopting a specialized, system-driven approach in your medical practice frees you to focus on patient interactions and high-level decision-making, which are the heart of patient care. These strategies, supported by real-world examples and actionable tools, provide a blueprint for transforming your practice into a more efficient and patient-centred operation. This chapter aims to equip you with the knowledge to enhance your operational efficiency, enabling you to dedicate yourself to what truly matters — your patients.

Chapter - 2

Expanding Your Reach

Expanding your patient base is crucial for the growth and sustainability of your medical practice. This chapter outlines several proven strategies for increasing your visibility, enhancing your reputation, and building trust within your community.

Leveraging Digital Marketing

Digital platforms offer powerful tools to connect with potential patients:

- **Social Media:** Platforms like Facebook, Instagram, and LinkedIn are not just for networking but also for educating the public and promoting health services. A 2020 study by Pew Research found that 80% of internet users search for health information online, including on social media.

- **Online Reviews:** Encourage satisfied patients to leave positive reviews. According to a 2021 healthcare survey, 72% of patients say they use online reviews as the first step in finding a new doctor.

- **Personal Website:** Develop a professional website that serves as a digital front door to your practice. Ensure it is informative, user-friendly, and updated regularly with health tips, blog posts, and practice updates.

Incorporating SEO Best Practices

Optimizing your online content for search engines can significantly increase your visibility:

➢ **Keyword Research:** Identify and use relevant keywords that potential patients might use when searching for healthcare services.

➢ **Quality Content:** Regularly update your website and social media platforms with high-quality, informative content that addresses common health concerns and showcases your expertise.

Networking with Other Professionals

Building a referral network can significantly expand your patient base:

➢ **Referral Programs:**

Partner with medical professionals of other specialties who can refer patients to your practice. Offering reciprocal referral agreements can enhance these partnerships.

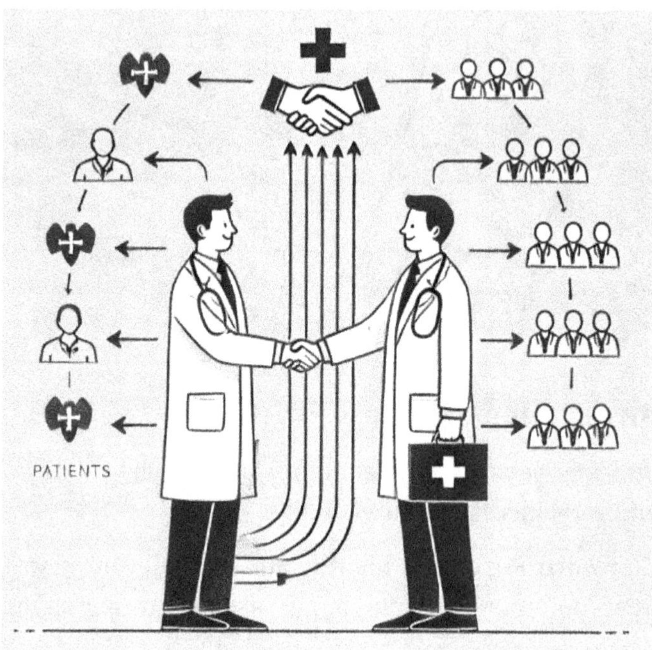

➢ **Community Health Events:**

Participate in health fairs, seminars, and workshops. These events position you as a trusted authority in your field and enhance community engagement.

Case Study: Successful Referral Program

A consultant in North-East India established a referral partnership with local specialists and saw a 25% increase in new patient visits over six months. His strategy included regular communication with partners and providing them with detailed information about his areas of expertise.

Educational Content

Educational content establishes your authority and helps build trust with potential patients:

➢ **Blogging:** Share insights on relevant health topics. Blogs can improve your website's SEO, drawing more visitors.

➢ **Videos:** Create and share videos that address common health concerns. Videos are highly engaging and can significantly increase patient understanding and comfort with your practice.

Offering a Unique Value Proposition

Highlight what sets your practice apart, such as:

- **Specialized Services:** If you offer unique treatments or technologies, highlight these in your marketing materials.

- **Patient-Centered Care:** Emphasize a patient-centred approach in all communications to make prospective patients feel valued and respected.

Patient Experience

Ensuring an exceptional patient experience can turn satisfied patients into advocates for your practice:

- **Quality Care:** Ensure that every patient interaction is positive, from the first phone call to the follow-up after a visit.

- **Engagement:** Keep patients engaged with regular updates, health tips, and personalized messages.

Case Study: Enhancing Patient Experience

A Neuro-Psychiatric clinic revamped its patient interaction strategy by training staff in customer service excellence and implementing a personalized follow-up system. This approach led to a 27% increase in patient referrals.

Host Free Workshops or Webinars

Offering free educational sessions on topics relevant to your specialty can attract people interested in those areas and introduce them to your practice.

Corporate Connections

Build partnerships with local businesses to offer their employees special consultations or health checks at special corporate rates. This can broaden your patient base and strengthen community ties.

Traditional and Digital Advertising

While digital marketing is crucial, traditional methods like print ads, radio spots, and community bulletin boards remain effective, particularly in reaching certain demographics.

Conclusion

By integrating these strategies, doctors can effectively enhance their practice's visibility, establish credibility, and attract new patients. The integration of real-life case studies and statistics provides a solid foundation for these recommendations, while suggested visual elements help illustrate these concepts clearly, making the information more accessible and engaging.

□ □ □ □

Chapter - 3

Building a Strong Foundation

Creating a solid foundation in your medical practice is not just a business strategy—it's a commitment to provide a warm and welcoming environment that you value and recognise every patient's visit. This chapter explores the essential elements that help create a professional yet comfortable atmosphere where patients feel genuinely cared for the moment they step into your clinic.

The Power of First Impression

The importance of first impressions in healthcare cannot be overlooked. Research shows that the initial minutes of a patient's visit can significantly influence their overall satisfaction and their decision to continue their care with you. This is why the first face they see is the reception staff who plays a crucial role.

➢ **Warm Reception:** Ensuring that reception staff are not only welcoming but proficient in customer service. They should be well-equipped to handle various patient interactions with empathy and efficiency, making each patient feel seen and respected.

> **Comfortable Waiting Area:** This space should feel like calming and soothing, where patients can feel at ease. Comfortable seating, soothing decor, and a clean environment contribute to a calming atmosphere that can ease patient anxiety.

> **Overall ambience:** The design, artwork & graphics of the clinic area have an emotional impact on patients. It has been clinically proven that certain art actually helps patients recover faster. Plus, art positively affects your staff, who see it every day.

Case Study: Reception Transformation

A clinic that focused on improving its reception experience saw remarkable results. By investing in customer service training for their staff and redesigning the waiting area to be more welcoming, they achieved a 28% reduction in patient complaints and a significant increase in overall satisfaction ratings.

Enhancing Patient Comfort and Trust

Building trust with patients goes beyond medical treatment; it starts with how they are treated the moment they walk through your door.

➢ **Clear Communication:** Keeping patients informed about what to expect during their visit, including wait times and token numbers, is vital. Effective communication can help in building trust and reducing patient stress. It shows that you respect their time.

➢ **Amenities:** Offering amenities such as spotlessly clean restrooms, drinking water, complimentary refreshments, and Wi-Fi access can make the waiting time more pleasant and show that you care about their comfort.

Training Staff in Customer Service

A well-trained staff is the backbone of a thriving medical practice. Investing in comprehensive customer service training can transform the quality of care provided and enhance patient loyalty.

➤ **Empathy and Listening:** Training should emphasize the importance of empathy and active listening, ensuring that staff fully engage with and understand patient concerns.

➤ **Managing Situations:** Equip your team with the skills to handle challenging interactions diplomatically and professionally.

➢ **Consistent Service Standards:** Develop and maintain high service standards that all staff members are trained to meet, ensuring a uniformly excellent patient experience.

Case Study: Staff Training Success

A healthcare centre implemented an extensive customer service training program for all frontline staff. The results were striking—a 48% increase in patient satisfaction and a significant rise in patient referrals, illustrating the direct benefits of skilled communication and empathetic service.

Establishing a Caring Environment

Consistently excellent patient experiences are built on a foundation of genuine care and respect.

➢ **Regular Feedback:** Implement a feedback system to actively solicit and respond to patient input. This shows that you value their opinions and are committed to continuous improvement.

➢ **Celebrating Success:** Regularly recognize and celebrate staff success who excel in providing exceptional care, fostering a culture of pride and dedication in your team.

Conclusion

Establishing a strong foundation in your medical practice is about much more than aesthetics and processes—it's about cultivating an environment where patients feel valued, respected, and cared for. By implementing these human-centred strategies, enhanced with real-world examples and visual aids, you can significantly improve the patient experience and set the stage for a successful, thriving practice.

□ □ □ □

Chapter - 4

Stay in Touch

Maintaining ongoing communication with your patients is crucial for building long-lasting relationships and ensuring they feel continuously supported in managing their health. In any business, communication is the key to maintaining healthy relationships with customers, and medical practice is no exception. This chapter probes into effective strategies for staying in touch with patients, enhancing their loyalty, and encouraging proactive engagement with their healthcare.

Leveraging Technology for Effective Communication

➢ **WhatsApp Messaging:** WhatsApp is the most commonly used app in India, and it is a very convenient way to send reminders directly for upcoming appointments and follow-ups for regular health checks. These messages can be automated based on the patient's care schedule, ensuring they receive timely nudges to manage their health proactively.

➢ **Email Newsletters:** Regular newsletters help keep patients informed about the latest health tips, practice updates, and new services or technologies. They can also be used to send targeted health campaigns based on patient age, condition, or past visits. Tools like Mailchimp provide user-friendly interfaces for crafting visually appealing emails that can include interactive content such as links to new blog posts or videos.

Personal Touch: Beyond Digital Communication

➢ **Personal Calls:** Making follow-up calls to patients, especially those with complex or unique medical conditions, to check on their recovery and clarify any post-visit instructions adds a personal touch to the care experience. These calls not only make a significant impact on patient well-being but also provide profound professional satisfaction.

➢ **Customized Health Plans:** Developing personalized health plans based on a patient's specific health data can greatly enhance patient engagement. For example, a diabetes or cardiac patient might receive a customized diet and exercise plan along with regular check-in prompts through their preferred communication method.

Community and Patient Engagement

➢ **Health Workshops and Webinars:** Hosting educational sessions on topics like nutrition, exercise, chronic disease management, and mental health can create awareness among the community. Platforms like Zoom or Google Meet can also facilitate these events, allowing people to join from anywhere.

> ➢ **Social Media Interactions:** Regular engagement on platforms such as Facebook, Instagram, or YouTube can keep the community connected to your practice. Live Q&A sessions, health challenge posts, and educational videos on the latest in health care can foster a vibrant online community. This helps in creating authority in the communities.

> ➢ **Free Health Checkup Camps:** Organizing free health checkup camps in local communities and rural areas can significantly enhance community trust and engagement. These camps provide essential health services to underserved populations and offer an opportunity

for direct interaction with potential new patients. By providing valuable healthcare services at no cost, you not only aid in improving public health but also demonstrate your commitment to community well-being.

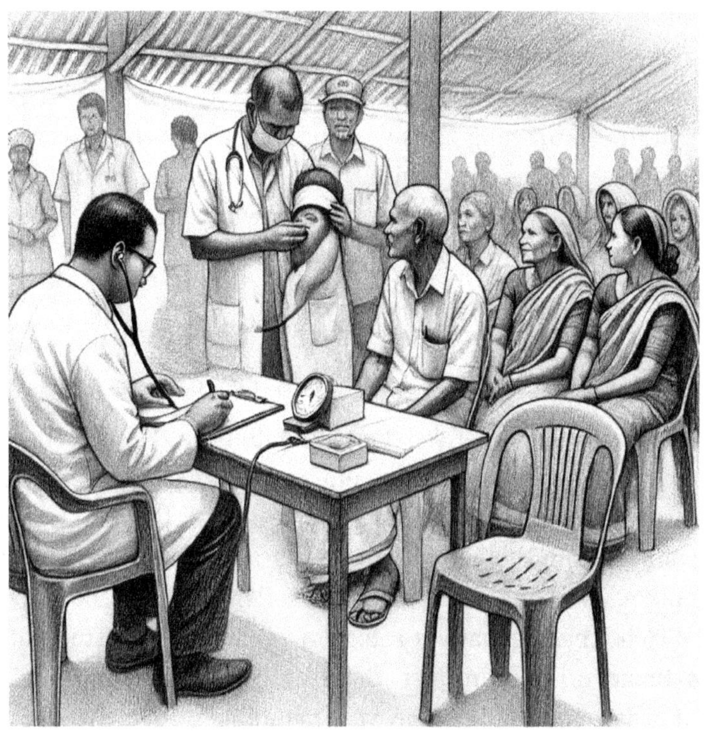

Celebrating Health and Appreciation

➢ **Annual Health Celebrations:** Designating specific days for awareness on important health topics on various World health days can be a catalyst for community screenings, special newsletters, and social media campaigns aimed at raising awareness and offering preventive screenings.

Conclusion

By effectively utilizing these communication strategies and engagement activities, you can build a supportive and interactive relationship with your patients. This not only improves their health outcomes but also enhances their overall satisfaction with your practice. This chapter has outlined various methods and provided examples to guide you in establishing a robust communication framework that integrates technology with a personal touch, ensuring your patients feel valued and cared for at every step of their health journey.

Case Study: Boosting Patient Engagement with Personalized Communication

A medical practice implemented a comprehensive communication strategy to enhance patient engagement. By integrating automated WhatsApp reminders for appointments, sending monthly email newsletters with health tips, and making personalized follow-up calls, the clinic observed a 30% increase in patient retention and a 25% boost in patient satisfaction within just three months. This personalized approach not only improved patient engagement but also resulted in better health outcomes and strengthened the patient-clinic relationship.

□ □ □ □

Chapter - 5

Empathetic Healthcare

Empathy is fundamental in healthcare, serving not just to enhance the relationship between patients and providers but also to significantly improve clinical outcomes. This chapter discusses how integrating empathy into your practice can profoundly improve patient care and satisfaction, supported by proven strategies, research findings, and real-life examples.

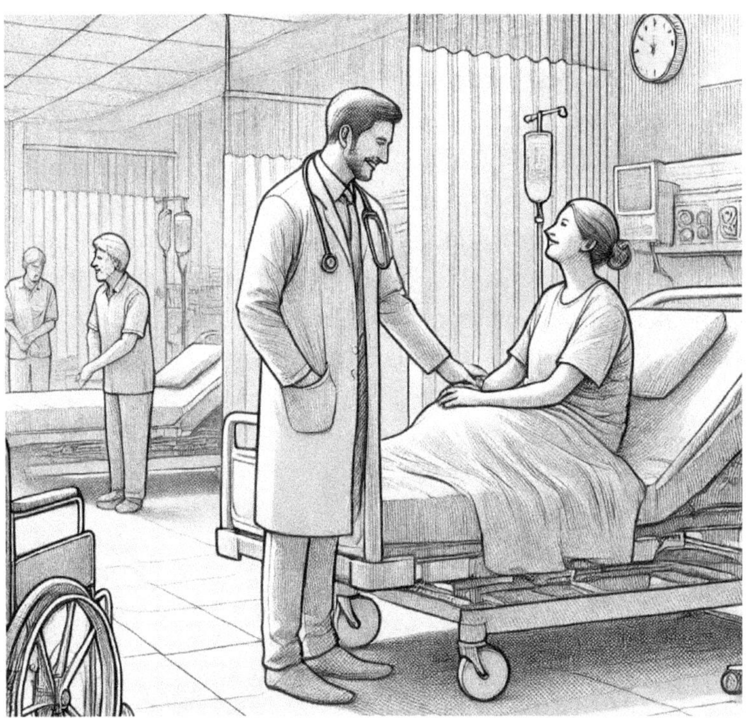

The Importance of Empathy in Patient Care

Understanding and sharing the feelings of others, empathy in healthcare means acknowledging both the emotional and physical needs of patients and addressing them with genuine care and compassion. Research shows that empathetic healthcare practices lead to better patient compliance, reduced stress levels, and significantly higher satisfaction. A study published in the *"Journal of General Internal Medicine"* in 2020 highlighted that healthcare providers rated highly for their empathetic care saw a 50% decrease in patient dissatisfaction and a notable 20% increase in adherence to prescribed treatments.

The "Customer is God" Philosophy

In many cultures, particularly in India, there is a deep-rooted tradition of treating the customer as sacred, known as "Grahak Devo Bhava" (ग्राहक देवो भव) or "Customer is God." This principle is particularly powerful in healthcare, stressing the utmost respect and prioritization of patient needs. When healthcare professionals adopt this philosophy, it not only enriches patient relationships but also sets a high standard for care that is deeply patient-centred.

Cultivating Empathy Through Communication and Practice

> **Active Listening:** This essential skill involves paying full attention to the patient, understanding their concerns, responding thoughtfully, and retaining the information shared. This type of engagement helps build trust and a stronger connection between the patient and healthcare provider. This goes beyond medical treatment to include empathy, respect, and a supportive environment.

➢ **Patient-Centred Communication:** Every patient comes with a unique set of circumstances and health issues. Adapt communication to fit the individual needs of patients.

➢ **Building Trust and Credibility:** Trust is the foundation of any doctor-patient relationship. Being transparent about treatments, procedures, and costs helps build this trust. Additionally, consistently delivering high-quality care and showing genuine concern for patient welfare enhances the credibility.

➢ **Accessibility and Convenience:** Making the practice as accessible and convenient as possible. This can include offering flexible scheduling, minimizing wait times, and using technology to streamline appointments and follow-ups. A patient-centric approach means making every interaction a positive and pleasant experience.

➢ **Empowering Patients:** Providing patients with education and resources empowers them to make informed decisions about their health. This could be through informational brochures, workshops, or digital content. An informed patient is more likely to feel in control of their health journey, leading to better outcomes and satisfaction.

➢ **Acknowledging and Respecting Patients:** Small gestures of acknowledgment, like greeting patients by name, celebrating their milestones, or simply expressing gratitude for choosing you, can make a big difference. Respect for their time, privacy, and individual preferences is also paramount.

➢ **Special Offers on Your Special Days:** On special days like your birthday, wedding anniversary, kids' birthday, work anniversary etc., various services can be offered at discounted prices or some free services to the patients. This will not only help to retain patients but also build a strong bond and also get a chance to receive their blessings on special days.

Assessing the Effectiveness of Empathetic Practices

➤ **Patient Satisfaction Surveys:** Implementing a system for collecting and acting on patient feedback is crucial. This not only helps in identifying areas for improvement but also makes patients feel valued and heard. Regularly updating your practices based on patient feedback demonstrates a commitment to excellence and patient satisfaction.

➢ **Follow-Up Calls:** Routine follow-up calls to check on patients' post-visit wellbeing not only provide continued support but also offer another opportunity to gather feedback and reinforce the caring nature of your practice.

Case Study: Improving Patient Care Through Empathetic Practices

A healthcare practice enhanced its empathetic approach by implementing patient satisfaction surveys and routine follow-up calls. Feedback from the surveys helped identify areas for improvement, leading to adjustments in service delivery. Follow-up calls provided continued support and allowed the practice to address any post-visit concerns. These initiatives significantly improved patient satisfaction and reduced complaints, demonstrating the positive impact of empathy-driven practices on strengthening patient relationships and enhancing care quality.

Conclusion

Incorporating empathy into every aspect of patient care is both a moral obligation and a practical approach that yields improved healthcare outcomes and enhanced patient satisfaction. This chapter offers a comprehensive guide on building an empathetic environment within your practice, supported by tangible examples and actionable advice. By embracing the philosophy of "Customer is God" and prioritizing empathy, your practice can achieve significant advancements in patient care and forge stronger, more trusting relationships with patients.

Conclusion

The book contains detailed strategies for doctors to enhance their medical practices. It covers essential topics such as creating a welcoming clinic environment, effectively communicating with patients, utilizing digital marketing for broader reach, maintaining strong patient relationships through personalized care, and adopting a patient-first approach to healthcare. The guidance provided aims to improve patient satisfaction, streamline clinic operations, and promote both professional growth and satisfaction for healthcare providers. These insights empower doctors to focus on delivering high-quality care while also managing the business aspects of their practice efficiently.

□ □ □ □

A Note of Support and Success

Dear Esteemed Doctors,

This book has been written with a deep respect for the work we do and the people we serve. Over the past 28 years, the lessons I've learned and the experiences I've gathered have shaped this guide. It's meant to help you streamline your operations, reach more patients, and build stronger relationships.

Each strategy presented here comes from real challenges and solutions—tested and proven in the field. By adopting these approaches, you're not just improving your practice; you're enhancing the quality of care you provide.

If the strategies and insights within this book relate to you and you're considering implementing them, we would love to hear your feedback. As a reader of this book, should you require any support with implementation, or if you're looking for personalized strategies to further elevate your practice, please don't hesitate to reach out. We're here to arrange a dedicated meeting to explore tailor-made solutions that align with your goals, ensuring our support becomes a cornerstone of your achievement.

Thank you for your dedication to health and for being part of this journey to uplift the standard of healthcare.

Best regards,

Kuljive Mahajan
kuljive@consernpharma.com

www.ingramcontent.com/pod-product-compliance
Lightning Source LLC
LaVergne TN
LVHW011308210726
843509LV00017B/2078